THE INDISPENSABLE GUIDE TO COPYWRITING

How to Write Effective and Compelling Copy That Sells

Helen Bolam

Independently Published

Copyright © 2020 Helen Bolam

All rights reserved

No part of this book may be reproduced, or stored in a retrieval system, or transmitted in any form or by any means, electronic, mechanical, photocopying, recording, or otherwise, without express written permission of the publisher.

ISBN-13: 9798572400052

Cover design by: Helen Bolam

CONTENTS

Title Page
Copyright
Copywriting, What's It All About?   1
Understanding the Product You're Writing About   8
Recognising Your Reader   18
Writing the Brief   23
Compose Your Copy   28
How to Write Headlines that Sell   29
How to Assemble Your Copy   35
Call to Action   41
Develop Your Copy   46
Be Innovative   47
How to Get Your Ideas Flowing Again   56
How to Captivate Your Reader   63
How to Polish Your Copy   69
Mastering the Art of Persuasion   77
How to Use Psychology to Engage, Influence and Sell   84
How to Hit the Right Tone   90
Hints and Tips for Various Projects   95
Tools   99
Tools and Resources to Make Your Life Simpler   100

Afterword

COPYWRITING, WHAT'S IT ALL ABOUT?

◆ ◆ ◆

Copywriting, not to be confused with copyright, is the ability to write words that sell.

Every time you pick up a magazine, read a paper, or click on an advertisement, that's all clever copy.

Copyright is something entirely different and simply means a company or individual has the legal right to publish, reproduce, or distribute someone's work.

Do You Need Qualifications to Be a Copywriter?

The simple answer is no, all you need is a laptop and internet connection to start your copywriting career. Learning from other copywriters through courses may also help you along the way.

Copywriting for Bloggers

Copywriting can be used in your content, helping your search engine rankings. It can also help build trust and awareness with your readers.

Things to think about when your copywriting:

1. Let Them Know You Can Make Their Lives Better

Whatever product you're trying to sell, you need to persuade your audience of the benefits your product offers. By simply arousing their curiosity, and attention, with the advantages your product offers, then winning them over with the details.

2. Be Constantly Building Relationships With Your Current Customers and New Customers

The only way your audience trusts you is through the words you write, you can do this through your tone and voice. Along with some other more effective techniques in order to create a connection.

Getting to know your audience first, is an effective way of presenting the benefits of whatever you may be selling. Your copy lays the foundation of, hopefully, what will be a long lasting relationship with your customers or followers.

Here are some simple steps for you to follow to build a relationship with your customers:

Use features of your product or service that will connect with your readers, and appeal to them on that level.

Always follow through and deliver on your products and services.

Always respond directly to any customer complaints, requests, praise and social media contact.

3. Less is More When Writing Copy that Sells

A huge misconception is that you need a page full of words to effectively get your message across. This is a great misconception of copywriting, your readers don't want to be bored to death, but instead give them short pithy paragraphs that get straight to the point. Including enough information about the vital information as they need.

4. Make Your Copy Easy-to-Read

Write easy digestible copy that your readers can quickly skim over, and lay it out using the following points:

Break-down long paragraphs into two or three short ones

Use numbered or bullet point lists

Make important text bold

Create interesting images to separate paragraphs or blurbs

The more interesting the information looks. the more likely people are to continue reading.

5. Always Make It About Them, Not You

Make your copy personal to your audience, that's the key to successful copywriting.

By writing a copy in a more conversational style, and telling an interesting story, you connect with your audience.

At the end of the day copywriting is all about persuading your audience, and understanding your audience's wants and needs. You do this by presenting them a product or service in the best possible light, that's the key to getting them to buy.

How to Write Really Great Copy

1. Familiarise Yourself With the Product

Understanding the product you're about to sell is paramount in the copywriting process.

By simply putting time to one side to study and learn your products' features, will help you understand how it will stand-out to customers.

If you're selling one of your own products or books you should already know about the products and features, as well as the workings and benefits your product will provide for the customer. This is a great foundation for any copy.

Write about what you know, instead of in-depth research, this will save you time in the long run, and help you to get more acquainted with your product.

Have a description ready, and save it in one place so that you always have a copy of it on hand.

2. Learn About Your Customers

Know your audience before you start selling to them.

If you know your audience you'll already understand what it is they want. This makes it all about the buyer, not the company.

Do Some Customer Research

Start by asking these questions:

Who are your customers?

What kind of customer is buying your product?

What does your regular customer look like?

What is it that customers like about your product?

3. Write Dazzling Headlines

Great copy rests on your headline.

Headlines are a *sprat to catch a mackerel*, because it doesn't matter how big or small your campaign is, if the headline is good enough it will catch the eye and reel in the consumer.

3 important points for writing awesome headlines:

1. A headline should be unique

2. A headline should be specific

3. A headline should carry a sense of urgency

4. Write Compelling Copy

Copywriting is the form of writing that persuades.

It doesn't take a wordsmith or literary genius to write great copy, but rather requires a series of steps that will convince your reader to buy.

Here are 8 tactics to convert readers into customers:

1. Give Your Visitor a Proposition They Can't Refuse

In findings from the Nielsen Norman Group you need to communicate clearly your value proposition within the first 10 seconds, otherwise you lose your customer.

Keep it simple and let your customer know what it is that you're offering. To achieve this try compressing the core of your product to only a few words.

2. Move On to the Benefits

What does the consumer get out of it?

You need to explain to your customers how your product will benefit them in the long run.

3. Expound on the Features

This is where you can tell the consumer about the features on offer with your product.

Do this in easy digestible chunks.

4. Write a Firm Call-To-Action

This is where you tell your reader what to do next.

Your call-to-action should be simple, and done in only a few words.

And if you're creating an email list, this should include your company's branding.

5. Create Scannable Content

You may have come across this already online, but people read differently when they're online to when they're reading offline.

This part is pretty simple, just remember to include bullet lists, headers and plenty of white space.

6. Write Using Persuasive Words

There are five words in the English language that will persuade anyone, and these are:

Instantly

Because

Free

You

New

Sprinkle these words in your copy and you should start seeing some really noticeable results in conversions.

7. Use Social Proof

Testimonials are a big favourite of most people selling, but you can also use:

Clients you've worked with

Number of followers or social connections

Subscriber counts

Media logos

Ratings

Use this step practically and include what you think is the best social proof to persuade your customers.

Simple points to remember:

4 Tips for Writing Great Copy

Tips for the Product Description - Describe Your Product in two or three sentences.

Point Out Any Unique or Special Features About Your Product - Your aim is to show the customer the uniqueness of your product or book.

How Will It Benefit the Customer? - Customers want to know not only about the product's uniqueness but also about the advantages it provides.

Does It Alleviate Pain? - Consumers buy for two reasons - to increase their pleasure or lower their pain.

What Kind of Features Does the Product or Book Have? - Make a list of all features the product has, and how each feature will benefit the customer.

UNDERSTANDING THE PRODUCT YOU'RE WRITING ABOUT

❖ ❖ ❖

Every piece of copy you produce is to sell a product.

Here are four things to look for when you're writing for a company:

Business-to-consumer product - e.g. bottle water, or trainers.

Business-to-consumer service - e.g. house insurance, or window cleaning.

Business-to-business product - e.g. pens, or a van.

Business-to-business service - e.g. social media marketing or accountancy.

Copywriting isn't just about writing for businesses and blogs, but also non-profit and charity organisations.

Many of the methods we'll be looking at will be about the reader helping somebody else, instead of helping themselves.

Rather than selling a product you might "sell" an idea, or opportunity, for example something simple like a job ad to motivate people to reply, because you want to encourage your reader to 'buy in' to what you're saying, or take steps other than making a purchase.

The copy you might be offering may be just information about an offer, or leaflet for the local job centre about how to claim working tax credit, or a piece of copy for a blog post about cleaning a car.

Figuring Out the Product

Before you can start writing you need to understand what it is you're trying to sell.

Here are some important points to consider:

What is the item?
How does it work?
Who can use it?
Are there any unusual or unique features?
What reason would people purchase this item?
Where do people have to go to purchase the product?
Is there a purchasing journey?
Is it a basic, regular, or premium product?
What is the item's situation in the market?
Does the product supersede anything else?
What are the other alternatives on the market?
If the product is already selling, what do people think of it?
If it's a service, how is it dispatched?
How do the history and culture of the organisation feed into the item on sale?

All of these questions are useful for a meeting with your client. The client may not have taken half of these points into consideration. If there are any points that you're not sure about, get it all down, because you can't go back for the information you might have missed.

Learning More About the Product

Other useful information you can get from the client might include; Brochures, web pages, internal presentations etc. If they already have their own notes, take it, but tell them basic numbered or bulleted points will be sufficient. All you are looking for is raw material, not a well-written document.

If you get the opportunity, test the product out for yourself, this may be more difficult if it's some kind of service or specialised product. You could also try talking to people who've used the product. You could do this via social media, and sending out a simple questionnaire, to get a feel for the item in question.

Talk to the Client Face-to-Face

Oftentimes you may actually get the opportunity to see the business and product for yourself, if the client decides they want to talk to you face-to-face. This is an ideal opportunity to get to know your client, but also build a relationship with the company for future projects.

This kind of visit is really beneficial for professional services, or a product you would find difficult to get a hold of.

During these important visits or chats on Skype, you can record the conversation for future record, and concentrate on what is being said.

Often you can take the simplest of phrases or truths about the company and use them in your copy. There may be some simple questions that still need to be asked, don't be afraid to ask them. That's what the client is there for.

There's No Such Thing as Too Much Information

When you're gleaning information about a product, it's often your first encounter with the product, this can give you a new perspective on how you perceive the product, it's a lot like the customer experiencing the product for the first time.

Unfortunately over time your point of view can change and you can have too much knowledge about the product or service. That's why a lot of businesses change creative agencies, so they can get a fresh pair of eyes to look at their product.

Recognise the Benefits

Learn how the features of a product explain the benefits, and which advantages are the best.

Details vs Advantages

Something to think about.

You're thinking about going on holiday, but all you can think about is a glitzy hotel on the Las Vegas strip, but my thoughts are for something a little quieter, a cottage on the Cornish coast.

What Can I Say to Change Your Mind?

I could start by telling you some useful information about the cottage:

It sits on Porthleven
It has WiFi
Its within 2 minute walk of the Ship Inn, a 17th century smugglers' haunt
It's got one bedroom

For me all of these things sound perfect, and I'm already convinced.

In order to get you to start thinking more like me, I need to convey the same points in a distinctive way to get your attention:

You can enjoy your coffee in the morning while your enjoy the surf
You can continue with your fitness routine and still have the time

to unwind
We can go out to dinner and be back home in 2 minutes

The first list is of the cottage's main facts and features, while the second list talks about its main advantages and benefits. That is to say, the first list is about the cottage, the second list tells you how it will help you.

Why Certain Advantages are Important

At the end of the day people like interesting things, even if it's an ad.

Everybody likes things that have a particular benefit in their lives. In order to get someone's attention you need to find their sweet spot, or something that will meet the reader's self-interest. Benefits are the core of powerful copywriting.

Your most valuable asset as a copywriter is your reader's attention, you begin with none, and take what you can get by not wasting it! Your reader will stand with you as long as you're offering them something real. If they can't understand the benefit they'll walk away.

The order you're going to sell your benefits in is a big part of planning your copy. You may be writing a print ad which is all about the benefits the product provides, on the other hand you could be writing a product description for a website which mentions a number of different benefits, but some of these will be asserted more than others.

Changing Features into Benefits

Benefits are a valuation of worth. When your customer uses the product they're the good things that happen.

Looking back at the features of the cottage, the words 'you' and 'your' were used all of the time because they define the relationship between the item bought and the consumer.

An important part of copywriting is to make all features of products beneficial, so the customer can see how products will relate to their life.

Here are some business to consumer examples of details and advantages they offer:

Winter Coat

Feature

Has a fleecy lining.

Benefit(s)

Keeps you warm and cosy in cold weather.

Breakfast Cereal

Feature

Full of fibre, high GI

Benefit(s)

Will keep you full all morning

A couple of examples for business to business:

New Website

Feature

Powerful design

Benefit(s)

Will respond to mobile technology no problem

Cleaning Service

Feature

All offices cleaned every night

Benefit(s)

Better hygiene, clean workspace

You could try putting yourself in the reader's shoes and asking yourself why different features are more beneficial for you.

You could start by asking basic questions like:

How does the service or product help me?
Why do I need it?

The basic things mentioned above are the foundation for good copywriting, without them you can lose touch with the product you're writing about.

Real and Intangible Benefits

There are benefits that are real and functional, giving the reader something they see and touch when they use the product. These are real benefits, usually including what the product does and what it can do. These are all facts that are used when the reader compares the product with other similar products.

Other benefits are more personal and play on the consumers' emotions. They are called intangible benefits, and they use the users emotions by making them feel more fashionable, attractive, or secure.

Even though these benefits only exist in the mind of the consumer they're still very real and can be used when needed in copywriting.

Real Benefits

Appeal to a person's logic
Take place in people's lives
Resolve problems

Are benefits that can be seen touched or measured

Intangible Benefits

Solicit emotion
Occur in people's heads
Create improvement in someone's life
Is something that can't be touched or seen

Here are a few examples of real and intangible benefits:

Smartphone

Real Benefits

Access to the internet
Make phone calls
Includes lots of useful apps

Intangible Benefits

Makes you feel connected to the world
Keeps you up-to-date
Makes you feel trendy

Intelligent Thermostat

Real Benefits

Saves money
Saves on fuel bills
Kinder to the environment

Intangible Benefits

Impress your friends and family that you're helping to keep the environment green.

Which Advantages are More Beneficial?

You'll find that most products you use offer both real and

intangible benefits, but how much of each you decide to use in your work depends on the product.

Things like insurance would most likely include real benefits, because people are looking for a product with real value.

People will choose unrealistic benefits, but will still use real benefits to defend their choice.

Think of the amount of times you've bought a product on impulse, but in reality you were trying to justify the reason you purchased the product.

Distinguishing Features (or Unique Selling Points)

There are unique products on the market that often offer a secret recipe, official endorsements, or brand named technology. These are called USP (or unique selling points) in the industry.

With these kinds of benefits you can make some eye-catching claims in your copywriting with keywords like 'cheapest', 'only', or 'best', as long as you can support your claim.

Many companies will use their product's unique selling points more than most. When writing copy try not to include a feature just because it's unique to the item. That's where the uniqueness comes into a product, you need to write clearly about what makes the product more unique than other items in the same category. Don't write something that you can't back up.

Each to Their Own

Often the product will offer particular benefits to different people, and the consumer and user aren't always the same people. There may be other people who may benefit from the product other than the buyer, and they may even have a contribution in the buying decision.

The success of a product often rests on the decision of both groups, the buyer and the user.

When Qualities of the Product Become Benefits

When the user has a natural interest in the qualities of the product you may not need to use them as benefits. For hobbyists such as photographers, you may talk about catching a special moment in graphic colour and needle point sharpness. Most people want to know why this camera is better than the one they own. This mostly comes to the camera's technical details. If you miss these points out you're missing the most important part.

Camera geeks love reading and analysing this kind of information, recognising they've made the best buying decision.

RECOGNISING YOUR READER

◆ ◆ ◆

Understanding Your Audience

You need to really understand what it is that your reader wants, and how they feel when they read your advertisement.

Who Are You Writing For?

When you're writing copy, you're not writing for everybody, just a handful of people that are genuinely interested.

When it comes to advertising you can't be all things to all people because you'll end up with no customers. Rather appealing to the people most interested and who will appreciate your product at the end of the day. These are the people who are easiest to persuade.

In order to communicate your message effectively you need to first understand then be understood. It stands to reason that if you don't know who your reader is you can't write for them. Or worse still, you may write copy for yourself that pleases you and not your client.

Here are some examples of how your reader might live:

1. Identify People by age, gender - People born after 1980, or women over 40.

2. Finances - Homeowners with income over £60,000 pa.

3. Interests - People who like playing computer games. People who play squash.

Three ways to consider how your reader lives, what they want and how they feel:

1. Identify readers by their buying habits - People who only buy from the high street. People who only buy second-hand cars.

2. Identify readers by their product knowledge - People who don't use the internet. People who have bought from the brand before.

3. Identify readers by the buying choices - People who only shop at Tesco. People who only wear Marks and Spencer clothing.

How many of these points you'll actually need will greatly depend upon the product you're writing copy about. A good example of this is a product such as kitchen roll. Most adults buy kitchen rolls so you'll need to narrow down your target audience.

There may be many digital projects that have points that determine the audience. Online ads are delivered through programmatic buying, which means the audience can be identified through known factors such as location, gender, age, or marketing emails sent using a particular profile of people, such as finance managers.

Particular products such as those aimed at the clothes and healthcare market, are also specifically pointed towards a particular group of people. Overall you can't base your copy on the reader's profile, avoid stereotyping your reader and defining your audience by terms like 'retirees' or 'housewives'. You need to look at how the reader wants and feels.

What Does Your Reader Desire?

From the outside you know how your reader looks, but what about the life they really live. What do they have going on right now? What new things do they want to bring into their lives and what do they want to get rid of?

Here are some options for business to consumer:

1. Have more free time.

2. Save money.

3. Get fit.

Here are some options for business to business:

1. Improve efficiency

2. Reduce overheads.

3. Build new skills.

Both of these options show that there isn't much difference between business to consumer and business to business readers.

Not all products require personal details to identify the reader, a good example of this is anyone wanting to get fit.

All of these examples show that not all readers will match up neatly with the product, or what it does.

Empathising with your reader

When you empathise with someone it's not enough to intellectually analyse how they act, but seeing what they see and feel. You need to take a leap of faith, realising that at the end of your experience it may have changed your life.

Researchers have found that pain and empathy are felt in the same part of the brain. That's why we literally feel pain when we empathise with someone.

When you empathise with someone you start respecting someone else's feelings, and start acknowledging their experience and their own personal reality. People start listening to you when you get down to their level.

Clearly it's impossible to listen to every single individual because you're building something that has to reach as many different people as possible.

Start thinking about some of these questions:

How does your reader perceive themselves now, or in the future?

How do other people see them? How do they think others perceive them?

What kind of person would they like to be?

What is it they want more or less of?

What do they look forward to in the future?

Do they have a problem that needs solving?

What could change their life and make it worse?

How do they see the world?

Empathy is something you should take very seriously. It should be at the core of what you do. If your reader doesn't share your beliefs they are unlikely to listen.

You don't want to force people into believing something, instead you want people to see things in their own way and want to buy.

Not all purchases are driven by emotion, often people just want to buy a product that does the job.

Examine the Reader

A simple way of getting to know a customer is by asking them directly. They'll tell you their real thoughts about the product, why they like it, how it helps them which helps you to empathise with them. You'll also hear the downside of the product and important things that need addressing. You could find a family member or friend who's also used the product

You may also find that people don't express their real thoughts about the product, and instead give a rational answer. It's important to think about what they say and do.

WRITING THE BRIEF

◆ ◆ ◆

What You Need to Know About the Copywriting Brief

The copywriting brief is the mission statement for your copywriting project, letting you know what you need to do and when to stop.

It acts like a barometer, and will help you evaluate your copy. It's your benchmark for any questions you may have about the project you've been given. It will answer questions like, 'Is this part of the brief, and does this answer the brief?' If you don't see any problems with your copy, that's okay. If you do then you need to read your brief again.

If your client agrees with your brief upfront, then you shouldn't have any major problems further down the line. Big copywriting projects can fall apart because different parties start disagreeing on various aspects of the brief that were never clarified in the copywriting brief.

Components of a Copywriting Brief

Do I Write the Brief?

This depends upon the client, they may prefer you to write a brief, or you may have some ideas written down already. In some cases they may expect you to take the lead. Either way, it's your job to obtain a valid brief, even if it means you have to write it out yourself.

You may be provided with a brief if you're working with an agency. If not you can always talk it through with your client. In the long-run it's fine, providing you get the information you need.

With smaller projects you'll remember the information more easily, without putting it down on paper. There may even be times when you feel it best to just press-on with the project. But still there's no harm in writing out a brief as reference, because it will help you to stay focused.

What to Expect in a Copywriting Brief

Below are some of the things you can expect to find in a copywriting brief:

Product or Service

The product, what is it?

What kind of person is it for?

What does the product do?

By what method do people buy and use it?

Advantages

How will the product benefit people?

What advantages does it have?

Customer

What is your customer demographic?

In what way do they live?

What are their needs?

What are their feelings?

What are their thoughts on or about the product?

Are they currently using a similar product?

Intention

What do you want your readers to do, think or feel after reading your copy?

What position will they be in when they read it?

Plan

How will the copy be used? (Web page, YouTube video, sales letter,)

How long will it be? (75 words, 5 pages, 25 seconds etc)

How will it be arranged? (Calls-to-action, main title, sidebars, subtitles, etc)

Is there extra content to be added? (Music, diagrams, video, images, etc)

Pitch

What tone will the copy have? (laid back, energetic, emotional, light-hearted, serious, etc)

Barriers

Is there a maximum or minimum length?

Is there anything that should be included or left out?

Are there any legal issues (Trademarks, prohibited words, or regulations on scientific or health claims, etc)?

How does this copy fit in past projects, or those that will be written in the future?

Will it form part of a campaign, and used with similar ideas, and used in the future?

Will it be translated and appear in other countries?

Are there any SEO points to consider (Popular search terms that should be seen in the title etc)

Are there any guidelines to follow with regard to branding and voice?

More background information about the product

Information about the product (Technical specifications, development history, retail buying processes, buying channels, and marketing strategy)

Position of the product in the market (It's price point, any offers and discounts, how the customer perceives the product, and competitors)

What is the target market? (Customer profile, size, history, marketing persona)

About the client (History, culture, current setup, people, values)

About the brand (History, values and positioning)

Project management details

Timescale for copy (drafts, dates for copy plan, feedback, final copy, etc)

Where will the feedback come from and how will you receive it?

Who will endorse the final copy and how will you receive it?

How will your copy be delivered?

The Example Brief

Create a 750-1000 word web page to promote Ben Nevis bespoke conservatories and 'Ready Made Rooms'.

Targeting retired and middle aged owners with disposable income and savings who live in older homes. Who are looking into double glazing to improve the look, soundproofing, and energy economy of their homes. They want to leave their home to their children, the property value is a very important part of what they require from the product and service provided.

They don't like flashy sales people, and don't appreciate cowboy builders or companies. When they buy a product they want to feel like they've made a wise choice. They appreciate good service, and want to be treated with courtesy and care. They've probably never purchased a conservatory before, so they won't know the process involved.

Describe why Ben Nevis is beneficial in principle, and why Ben Nevis products are expertly superior. Reveal Ben Nevis' strong market position (ranked second by sales), the affordability of products and the extent of the range of products available. Relate the service step-by-step, and describe how the entire process is easy and flexible. Mention the 30-day money-back guarantee along with customer testimonials.

Recommend people to fill in the online form and request a quote, including calls-to-action throughout the web page. Utilise pullouts and subsections to impress skim-readers.

COMPOSE YOUR COPY

HOW TO WRITE HEADLINES THAT SELL

◆ ◆ ◆

So What is a Headline?

Your copy starts with a headline at the top of the page, this headline can also appear as:

A slogan of a poster or magazine advert.

Subject of an email.

Title of a blog post.

Main heading of a web page.

Marketing headlines are no different, they still have the same job of grabbing the reader's attention. Father of advertising David Oglivy, discovered that five times as many people read the headline, as read the body copy. It pays to leave extra time for your headline, because this is the only time you might catch your audience's attention. Billboards and posters depend upon a good headline, because that's all there is.

Even the most experienced copywriter will find headline writing difficult, which is why many copywriters make the body copy their priority, going back to the headline later on.

Quick note: Have a list of ideas, before you decide on the main headline.

Say What the Product Is

The best place to start is by telling your audience in the simplest way possible what the product is all about.

Example:

Amazon Audible

Find your next great listen from the world's largest selection of audiobooks.

This particular strategy is both direct and plain-speaking to your readers. Who can make the decision of whether they want to read on or not. There's nothing underhanded or dishonest about this notable approach.

No matter what your aim is, a good straight description will complement any SEO strategy, helping your web page reach the top of the pile on Google.

Determine the Theme

Headlines should grab a reader's attention, and should be a conversation starter. This will enable your audience to know that the copy is specifically for them.

Headlines aren't for everybody, and shouldn't grab everyone's attention. This will leave you with an empty headline and no attention. Instead, you should only hook the readers who share a particular interest in what you have to say.

The tone should be established straight away, which means any suggestion you give your audience, whether it be dark, businesslike, or jokey should carry on through the body of the text. This will set the pitch for the whole copy, letting them know what your message is, and set the mood for the whole copy text.

Buffer's login page is an example of a theme-setting headline:

Build your audience and grow your brand on social media.

Plan, collaborate, and publish thumb-stopping content that drives meaningful engagement and growth for your brand.

Instantly you can see this page is aimed at content creators, and website owners wanting to grow their brand and engage with their audience. Everyone else will just tune out, and disengage.

Suggest an Advantage

Every reader wants to know what's in it for them? This is the point where your reader is wondering if they should read on. In the same way that a book cover advertises a book, a headline is the ad for the advert.

A simple way to draw your reader in is by suggesting an advantage or benefit, and tell them 'There's something you might like, can I tell you about it?'. Self-interest will spark interest and hook your reader straight away. Which is why they work so well.

One benefit is enough for your feature, anymore and it's overkill. You can mention a few more at the bottom of the copy, but don't overdo it.

Keep Readers Reading

A key part of copywriting is the ability to create intrigue, the kind that keeps the reader absorbed. If you can do this up until the end of your copy you're doing just fine.

Offering your audience a benefit is a tried and tested way of drawing them in, but may not always be the best way to go. Another less direct way of getting your readers attention is the less direct route. You give them something that will pique their interest enough to want to read more. This can be done by revealing giving them more details that follow on from the headline.

Example:

Low Battery

The words you don't want to see the morning of a major pitch, when the final details are being done via email. Any hope of closing the deal rested with the battery of my phone.

If I'd only heard about the Anker Powercore battery pack sooner, and had it with me in my briefcase. I could have visited London ten times, and written as many emails.

With this particular method, speculating short-term relevance, with the hope of winning over long-term interest. 'Low battery' doesn't tell the reader anything about the product, but it does talk directly to the audience's previous experience. If that risk works, your audience will be more engaged and interested if they had been faced with a simple headline like 'Phone charging in motion'.

Question Your Audience

Questions only work if the audience answers them the way you want them to.

The easiest way to do this is by asking a leading question that will encourage a yes/no response.

Want to save money on your car insurance?

This is just a long winded way of saying 'Save money on your car insurance'.

Don't use too many questions because your reader will soon start to feel harassed and switch off.

If you start with 'what' or 'how', these questions will cause your reader to reflect more deeply on themselves and their situation.

Questions like 'who knows' means there's no need to answer.

When questions like this are used they usually spark fascination and mystery around the product. If the question isn't answered, you'll probably get a 'who cares?' answer.

Define Why

This is a good place to start if your product needs explaining before you start selling to your audience. Your body copy delivers the sell, while your headline provides some interesting and useful knowledge.

When you use the word 'Why' it gives your reader insight and information into the product. Giving your audience a deeper knowledge, rather than a myriad of facts.

Use Your Headline to Break the News

Readers are promised information and benefit from the power of a good news headline. It also counteracts their impulse to say 'not interested'. When the product you're offering is brand new, your audience needs to know more before they know it's for them.

Novelty appeals to everyone, but newness isn't like sameness, unless your reader is totally happy with what they're already using.

Here are some useful words you can use to break the news to your readers:

discover, now, new, and introducing.

Give an Instruction

Tell your reader what to do, and link your intention to your copy.

Instructions like these are a powerful tool to use in copy, because we don't hear them in normal life. Commands are usually only given out to military personnel, and used in a more gentle manner by managers and bosses at work.

A call to action can be used to instruct your reader, and in your copy headline.

Nike® is famous for its command which could be seen as inspirational, and an invitation to its customers to accomplish more.

Just Do It.

Nestlé Kit Kat® isn't as aggressive, as they simply encourage their audience to do something they like doing.

Have a Break, Have a Kit Kat.

HOW TO ASSEMBLE YOUR COPY

◆ ◆ ◆

Why You Need to Assemble Your Copy

When you're putting together your copy you need to give it order and meaning, otherwise it will have no foundation to stand-on. A well structured piece will help you get your point across to the reader in a coherent manner, enabling the reader to have a more pleasing experience, and solidifying your message in their mind.

We're going to look at a number of different ways to assemble your copy, helping you choose a plan to suit your copywriting purpose.

Create a Strategy

For most people jumping straight in might seem the best option when copywriting, but this can often end with a confusing message that doesn't get the right message across.

When you make a plan you understand where your copy needs to go, and what it needs to accomplish in the long-run. Making it a more efficient and productive piece of text.

A good place to start is by making notes about all of the top ranking ideas you want to cover. All of these will be made into a paragraph in your final draft. You might find it useful to write these on sticky notes or scraps of paper. Once you've written down all of your ideas, start assembling them in a logical manner, so that they make more sense.

Subheadings can be used for longer sections of writing so that you can divide them into broader areas and create more distinct fields.

It's best to just stick to planning and nothing else, because none of your words will go into the final copy. If your mind starts thinking about particular words and phrases, place them on separate notes for later on, then get back to your plan. At this stage we're just matching ideas together.

Make a Steady Start

Following the headline your opening is the next most essential part of your copy, and nearly as challenging to write. It needs to bring the reader in and have the desire to keep reading on, and demonstrate you're going to deliver on the promise of your headline.

You could try:

Asking a question.

Writing a story.

Linking to the reader's situation with if this then that.

Write a metaphor.

Suggesting something the reader already knows and linking to it.

Begin at the Middle First

You could try leaving your opening until later instead of attempting to write it first.

Start by pinning down the meaning of your copy, this usually includes the portion about the advantages of the product. Begin writing your headline, and determine how you'll get the reader through the text to the advantages the product has to offer.

Lastly connect to your call to action with some compelling points.

Similarly you could try writing a placeholder opening that doesn't quite fit into your copy on the understanding that you'll get back to it later.

Copywriting Formulas

Google is awash with copywriting formulas, so instead of letting you Google one let's take a quick look at a simple one right now.

FAB - Features - Advantages - Benefits

Features - What your product can do.

Advantages - Why is the product so helpful?

Benefits - What it means to the reader.

To put it simply: You get this...and the product does this...so that you get this.

This particular copywriting formula focuses on the benefits of a product, and not the features.

Fix a Problem

Use the product you're writing copy for as a solution to a problem, this is a sure-fire way of structuring your copy.

Keep it simple and focus on one problem (or *pressure point*) that may be troubling to the reader. Present the headline with the problem and perhaps the solution. In the body copy talk in further detail, before describing how the product solves the problem.

If you're writing a sales letter or landing page you may need to establish your credibility as a writer. You do this with a *Who I am* or *why you should listen to me* section.

Offer Information

All of your readers are at different stages of knowledge about the product you're trying to sell through your advertisement, this means you need to determine which stage this is before you start writing.

In the book *Breakthrough Advertising*, **Eugene Schwartz broke down prospect awareness into five distinct phases:**

1. The Most Aware: Your reader knows the product, and only needs to know the deal.

2. Product-Aware: Your reader knows what you sell, but isn't sure it's right for him.

3. Solution-Aware: Your reader knows the result he wants, but not that your product provides it.

4. Problem-Aware: Your reader senses he has a problem, but doesn't know there's a solution.

5. Completely Unaware: No knowledge of anything except, perhaps, his own identity or opinion.

You'll find that most copy is usually aimed at the middle three kinds of reader: *problem-aware*, *solution-aware*, and *product-aware*. The first two (*problem-aware* and *solution-aware*) usually take the pattern of problem solving, which emphasises the readers' situation, before going on to tell them about how things could be different if they used this particular product.

Don't spend too much time fixing the problem, instead tell them what they need to know and why this specific item is the one they should choose to solve their solution.

Once your reader has become product aware you can shift gears to convince them why they should purchase the product.

Useful Points to Consider When Writing Your Copy

1. Use a Different View Point

Everybody has a different viewpoint of the product, try speaking separately to different user groups that identify with your product.

2. Use the Family Tree Method

This method is usually used by newspapers and is a reliable way to give your copy a strong structure. You do this by starting with the central point, then gradually move on to the descending point in order of importance.

3. Try Making a List

If you've got a lot to cover, try making a list, this is particularly useful if you have a lot to say. You could start by listing the most important functions, using numbered subheadings.

4. Walk Your Reader Through Step-by-Step

With this system you walk your reader through the steps as a sequence or process, explaining each one in turn, like you were writing a recipe.

Making it ideal for the reader to understand something that may be a bit complicated before they commit to a sale.

5. Use the Magic of Three

If you live in the UK are of a certain age you're sure to remember Mars® bars catchy slogan:

A Mars a day helps you work, rest and play.

You can also apply this to sentences in a paragraph, because three sentences will be just enough to develop your argument without losing or boring your audience.

Only use rules when they're useful, and don't bother with them if

HELEN BOLAM

they're not.

CALL TO ACTION

◆ ◆ ◆

Call to Action Definition

an exhortation or stimulus to do something in order to achieve an aim or deal with a problem.

Oxford Languages.

Call to action centres on telling the reader what to do, they're the link between a reader being engaged or being dormant. Usually coming from the audience listening, reading or learning to do something in the moment. As a copywriter you laid out your claim, it's now time for the reader to take action. Which could be anything from purchasing a product, donating to charity, or contacting the company in question.

A call to action is usually found at the end of your copy, it might be at the bottom of an ad, sales letter, article, or at the end of an advertisement on TV. You can find them on printed media clearly marked showing the customer it's something separate from the rest of the copy, and it's something the reader needs to focus on and take action.

Online readers respond differently to calls to action. This is because a call to action can be something as simple as a link that needs to be clicked. The words used should help the reader understand what they're clicking on.

Here are some common online calls to action:

Sign up

Subscribe

Try for free

Get started

Learn more

Join us

Web pages are full of things to catch the reader's eye, so they're usually not in any kind of order. Which is why most calls to action can be found in the sidebar, in a pop up, or in a header at the top of the page so people don't miss them.

You can have a strong call to action, and weak content. Which is why it's important your call to action should feel like a gentle nudge to your reader asking them to do something they're ready to do.

Simple Call to Action

The most basic calls to action ask the reader to do something, so they usually come in the form of a command.

Here are some simple examples:

Claim your free trial

or they could be easygoing...

Call in any time for a quick chat

...or more persuasive...

Send me the coupons

Limited edition sign up now

Simple calls to action are usually short and to the point, and a good fit for circumstances where a reader may be easily distracted or where space is at a premium.

Introduce Advantages and Enticement

If you want to be more appealing, add an advantage, this will turn your call to action from an offer to a deal - 'try this today and you'll get this'.

Or:

To start downloading your free ebooks today simply sign up.

Don't create a new benefit, use a one you've already told your audience about. At this point your target is too close to a sale to not make your claim.

By using a more persuasive angle you can strengthen your call to action, for example telling the reader something is in short supply and that they need to act now or they'll lose out.

You only have 14 days to renew your subscription at this one-time only deal. Click here to secure your savings.

Social proof is another good way to show your audience that other people are already enjoying the advantages of the product:

Sign up and join thousands of other happy Skippy customers, by ordering yours from Amazon or other major online stores.

Make It Easy to Understand

Don't complicate it, keep it simple, with as few steps as possible. One is ideal, but if that is difficult, bring all of your points together to help the reader understand what they need to do, and the order they need to do it in.

To renew your passport, fill in this form, then bring it to any Post Office along with your old passport, a passport size photo and the £75.50.

Rather than using the same words over and over again, try varying them if you're writing copy for a website or a mailshot.

If your customer requires more than one choice make sure you include all of the options every time. Or use a general phrase to cover all of them (like 'Call us today').

Demonstrate How Easy It Is

Your audience needs to understand that whatever you ask them to do is easy. There should be little effort or thought about it, or a decision to be made. If you're showing them something new, they need to know what it is there getting into before they sign up or commit.

Your reader may be completely compliant with whatever you've written, but you're still asking them to take a step that will make a change, no matter how small or large. Most people don't like change, even if it's for something small.

Create Stepping Stones

You may not want to ask for a sale straight away, but instead gently guide your reader through their journey, or motivate them to read on.

Here's a good example of copy from an envelope sent by mail:

Open now and receive 20% off your next order at First for Fashion...

It's pretty clear that this statement isn't the complete story. The customer knows they need to do more than just open the envelope. This call to action is a simple way of making a connection with the action in order for the reader to get the advantage they'll gain in the end.

Just like any other kind of call to action, it's essential to make it clear what you require the reader to do, and what they'll receive in return, at each stepping stone. You should include a promise of some sort of value, and include the stage it leads to should fulfil that promise. It's worth pointing out that each call to action should only make reference to the next stepping stone, instead of jumping ahead to what the reader may do at a later time.

You could use stepping stones in another way to direct your readers through pages and sections in a particular order.

You could do this at the end of a webpage like this:

Read on or get in touch to talk through your project.

Not every visitor will follow through on this call to action, but the idea is still planted in their mind, and it leaves a more confident ending than just petering out at the end.

DEVELOP YOUR COPY

BE INNOVATIVE

◆ ◆ ◆

Why Do We Need to be Innovative in Copywriting, and How Does it Benefit the Reader?

The ability to create innovative copy is the core of good copywriting, and should be strived for at all times. Being able to produce creative copy that shows the customer the benefits of the product is top of the list when it comes to copywriting.

So how do you know real innovation when you see it up close?

The answer is split into three different parts:

1. Originality

When you write something that is original and creative, people will remember it because of its uniqueness, instead of a dull 'me too' message. This is because we're more likely to remember something that jumps off the page, than sits quietly in the background.

Well known copywriter Steve Harrison calls it 'relevant abruption', which is to say that it gets under the reader's skin, without the reader noticing it, making the reader even more intrigued.

2. Being Humorous

Being able to say what needs to be done in a humorous way that will make the reader laugh out loud. This is a considerate copy that requires subtlety, intelligence and intrigue that will leave your audience wanting more.

Creating humour makes your product less evident but more appealing, which requires the reader to pay more attention, allowing their brain to do the rest of the work. Their prize is twofold, understanding the message, and the satisfaction of working it out.

3. Being Emotive

Writing innovative copy allows you to write something that might be fun, exciting or aspirational. On the other hand this could also mean writing something that is mysterious, deep like love, or shows compassion. It could also be the complete opposite and be full of negativity, anxiety, or fear.

This is why ads that involve something close to home like ads for new parents, always appeal to the parents' love of their children. This may come into play if you're writing an ad for a charity, that style of writing brings out the best in people, and makes people feel emotional.

If you can make the reader feel strongly about something they're more likely to listen to your message and remember it. Be careful when you start bringing emotion into your copy, this could lead to more negative thoughts in the reader's mind.

Emotion, humour and originality are things you can dial up or down. Which means you can be as conventional, original, or unusual as you like. All of these things can be done in different combinations.

Imagination With Intent

Our culture is often enriched by the lessons learned in marketing, and is a reflection of the lives we live, a lot like art. While your copy is complete in its own right, marketing has a hidden agenda, whether it wants to tell you or not. Contrary to a Van Gogh or da Vinci, marketing wants to lure you in.

At the end of the day innovative copy is all about solving a problem you may have.

So What Does Your Innovative Copy Need to Do?

Ultimately your copy has a job that needs to be done, which comes in three parts: to answer your brief, amplify the benefits of the product, and most importantly sell the product.

Answering the brief means staying with the plan you were given, so you can aim your copy at the right reader.

Magnify the benefits and make them as appealing to your audience as possible.

Sell the product, which is the most important point of all. Your innovation has to be good enough to sell sell sell. You may get swept away in your ideas, and creativity, but all of this could be to your detriment, and be selling itself instead of the product.

Some Important Points for Innovative Copy

The process of innovation and creativity can be unclear at the best of times, so I'm going to help you out with 14 helpful starting points to get you started.

1. Make an Uncomplicated Start

When you start writing your copy, keep it simple and uncomplicated, addressing your reader in the simplest way you can think of. Stay clear of humorous dialogue, and originality.

For example:

Urban Apples is a light cider that is made in the UK, with only organic ingredients.

It is an artisan cider, quite light, with a unique taste that comes from the distinctive red apples grown in Northumberland.

Making a simple start gets rid of the blank page right off the bat, leaving you with the process of improving, and refining your editing process. Which is a lot easier when you already have words on the page.

2. Shake Things Up a Little

It may surprise you to know that most ideas aren't that new anymore; they're just new combinations of things that are already out there.

Or as Steve Jobs put it:

Creativity is just connecting things.

One of the best ways to spark creativity is to read and gather as much information as you can, then mull it over and let your subconscious mind do the rest.

3. Look at Things From a Different Angle

Looking at the product from a different angle will bring in new suggestions and ideas that are more effective things to write about, such as:

What would the product look like if its purpose was reused for a different purpose? Ask yourself things like how would a child use the product? Could it be mistaken for something else?

What would the product look like if it was distorted in some way? Made to look longer, or shorter etc?

What would the product look like if it was relocated to somewhere more exotic or exciting like the jungle, under the sea, was put in the past?

This kind of creative play leads to new thinking and fresh ideas, that may lead you to new places you hadn't thought of before. So don't knock playful thinking!

4. Use a Metaphor

Metaphors are used when you use a word or phrase and an object or action is applied. This helps if you're trying to explain something, not unlike a simile which takes a figure of speech and compares it to something else. You can use metaphors in your copy to connect the product with something familiar that the reader might know, enabling you to make light of some of the advantages of the product. For example:

When Was Your Last MOT?

If you're over 40, and male, your health is at risk of all kinds of problems. Make sure you make an appointment with your GP to keep you on the retirement road.

The human body doesn't share that many similarities to a car, but they both suffer from breakdowns and engine trouble, if they're not properly monitored.

This clever piece of copy creates a connection between something that may interest the audience (motoring), and something they might want to avoid (their own health).

If this kind of copy is too similar to the niche you're writing about, you might fare better with something more literal.

5. Provide a Contrast

Comparisons are great for highlighting similarities, contrasts on the other hand, can make light of differences. When contrasts are used in copy they normally convey some sort of tension going on between two things, at the same time solving them, creating a more equal message.

Contrasts have been used in car adverts, some campaigns have been more successful than others. This difference is seen clearly with the Toyota Yaris, and the Vauxhall Corsa.

Toyota Yaris

BigSmall

Vauxhall Corsa

The small car with the big personality.

The Yaris's message is more disjointed and doesn't really make much sense when you think about it. But the Corsa lays its cards on the table clearly and tells the reader in a way they understand.

6. Use Humour

When it comes to copywriting, humour is a way of really grabbing your audience's attention, while planting a message in their minds. It doesn't help that people will really like what you've written, which doesn't hurt either. Humour can help you lay out the product benefits in a very powerful way, as long as you stick to the script.

Your strokes can be broad or small, you can get straight or surreal, the main thing is that you're funny. You can give the product a unique twist by choosing a particular benefit and embellishing that. Just make sure you don't cross the boundary, because not everyone sees humour the same way you do.

7. Use Wordplay

When you start using wordplay you'll find it doesn't hold the same kind of wit that humour carries. Plenty of local businesses and small companies use wordplay, but it leaves nothing to the imagination, and can feel a little lacklustre.

Take a look at how Tesco has uses wordplay:

Freshly clicked.

This is used alongside a juice pyramid of tomatoes, or a bunch of asparagus. This clever phrase evokes a similar correlation between the 'freshly picked' tomatoes, and picking them from the supermarket shelf. Which also helps clear customers' concerns over outdated produce.

Always write your puns down, even if you think they're going to work or not as headlines, you may still have use for them at a later date.

8. Make Use of Images

Copywriting can often lie on visuals for the most impact. Not every advert requires words.

A useful modus operandi is to use one or the other, pictures or words, but not never both at the same time. That is to say that imagery, copy and words should only work together to communicate an idea. Copy isn't required if the image says it all, and vice versa. Images aren't required when your copy conveys it all.

9. Let the Reader Read Between the Lines

Sometimes what you want to say can only be interpreted by the actions seen. This allows you to involve the reader to create their own message, instead of just passing on information about the product, or telling them to buy it. You're telling the reader they need to join the dots instead of receiving the message passively.

The appeal of this kind of copy is to make the audience work harder. Unfortunately this kind of copy doesn't captivate every company you write for, but in the long term the reader will remember the message, as long as it's been well written.

10. Surprise People With the Opposite of What They Expect

You can do this by writing down all of the obvious things related to your product, then start writing down details that may be contrary to what you know about the product.

A good example of this is the campaign Harvey Nichols did 'Sorry I spent it on myself' shown on Christmas 2013. This showed people giving their relatives cheap presents, while they spent all of the cash on themselves. Most Christmas advertising is about giving, but this advert used greed and selfishness to make their competitors look saintly and quaint.

11. Different Equals Memorable

There's no harm in standing out from the crowd, especially when it comes to writing great copy. Things have changed quite a bit since the early days of advertising, when it was all fast trading. In the current climate marketing is all about 'staying home' and 'reassurance' to the local community and the world.

Here are some examples:

#KeepingtheUKConnected - **Vodafone.**

We're never lost if we can find each other - **Facebook App.**

I stay home - **Ikea®.**

Each of these adverts expressed perfectly the need for people to stay in doors, but some did that in a quirkier way than others. Like the Ikea® advert, added a sense of fun to staying home, the Facebook App ad told people they could be closer if they connected through their app.

Staying at home marketing campaigns have become the new norm, and is a long way from showing great sprawling scenes, with lush green forests, and wide open roads.

It's just a case of the angle you take, to make your copy different.

12. Serve a Curveball

Refashion your copy with a splash of humour, this can help amplify a benefit, and make people laugh along the way. Your story can be neatly woven together with the help of a little satire, and it will be an advert your audience will find hard to forget.

Ikea®'s #WonderfulEveryday campaign encourages people to think differently about their homes and 'Conquer the Great Indoors'. This is all put forward with a cuddly lion. They've turned long hours of staying indoors into something quite exciting with the help of their furniture. The curveball is the creation of 'the Great Indoors'. Who would have expected a house could look that exotic! It's pretty easy to see how furniture, and furnishings can become something exotic and out of the ordinary.

13. Create a Swipe File

Even the best copywriters run out of ideas at some point, so why not borrow from the best instead. No, that doesn't mean plagiarising someone else's work.

A 'swipe file' is a file full of well-known examples of work that copywriters like, that help to kick-start their writing flow. This is a commonly used tool in the industry, so it's nothing new.

When you start delving into other marketing campaigns you understand how problems have been solved in the past, making your job a little easier.

You can find answers in your own patch, and study current trends and styles. Companies big and small like to imitate each other's concepts, even if it's from a completely different industry, it might just work in your brief.

14. Go Further With Your Ideas

Chances are your ideas are only the start of a bigger picture, and the agency you're working for may be looking for more than just one idea. It only takes one good idea for your copy to be snapped up by a company.

Anyways, you need to have innovation at your fingertips, which is like a goldmine in the copywriting business.

HOW TO GET YOUR IDEAS FLOWING AGAIN

◆ ◆ ◆

Copywriters are under a constant amount of pressure to deliver the most amazing, gripping, irresistibly absorbing piece of copy ever.

But what really elevates a good copywriter above the rest is being able to generate the kind of ideas that define an ad campaign. This kind of idea making can transform a brand overnight, as well as define it, while changing the way people think about that particular product.

So what's the secret to generating these amazing ideas?

How to See Things Differently

How do writers come up with winning ideas everyday?

Copywriting is like any other skill in life, it's a discipline that allows copywriters to enter the zone of creativity. Whether they want to or not.

The scary truth that most writers and copywriters face regularly is that the well can run dry at the most inconvenient of times.

This usually happens at the worst moment, which could be a hanging deadline, dangling over your head like the sword of damocles.

So how do copywriters get their creative juices flowing again?

Here is a comprehensive list that pro-copywriters use to jump-start their creative juices and produce extraordinary ideas.

1. Learn to be a Lateral Thinker

What is lateral thinking?

the solving of problems by an indirect and creative approach, typically through viewing the problem in a new and unusual light.

According to Oxford Languages

This term was invented by Edward de Bono and this is what he had to say about it:

"With logic you start out with certain ingredients just as in playing chess you start out with given pieces. But what are those pieces? In most real life situations the pieces are not given, we just assume they are there. We assume certain perceptions, certain concepts and certain boundaries. Lateral thinking is concerned now with playing with existing pieces but with seeking to change those very pieces."

So how do you become more inventive with your ideas?

Here are some quick tips to get you started thinking laterally:

Problem solving

Many problems come with many obvious answers, so it can be useful to take some time to think laterally on the problem. This can be done by training your brain to think more naturally creatively, and help you to discover better solutions to your copywriting problems.

Discovering new ways

Most people are taught how to do things in a certain way, but there are other ways to do things in a more efficient and effective way. By using lateral thinking you can achieve not just your copywriting goals but also your writing goals.

Master your creativity

You can spend as little or as much time as you like thinking outside the box and trying things in a different way. If you can't answer your problem through lateral thinking, use your old way. As long as you use a portion of time to think laterally every once in a while, you'll do just fine.

2. Revise the Question

As I mentioned above, lateral thinking is about escaping conventions and preconceived ideas.

Try coming at your problem from a different angle, and throw away any preconceptions you have. In other words, revise or change the question.

3. Unlock New Possibilities

Most of the time we tie ourselves down by certain constraints and rules, but the reality is we're surrounded by new perspectives and possibilities, because many of these constraints are self-imposed.

Trying the same thing over and over again may not be very productive, but changing our direction altogether may bring something new to the table.

This perhaps is true in copywriting where flexibility and creativity are primary factors to idea generation.

Here are three take away points:

1. Understand your own perception.

2. Accept new perspectives.

3. Don't be bound by a problem - seek new solutions by defining the problem in a new way.

Sometimes thinking illogically can be the best thing you can do to solve a problem.

4. Do More Research

Preparation is key to any writing project you work on, so why would copywriting be any different.

If you're not properly prepared for the project in hand it will show, and will leave you staring at a blank page if your ideas aren't flowing.

You'll know that you've done enough research when you can't stop the ideas from coming out.

Your mind requires exercise and fuel, so fill it with as many ideas, concepts and theories as you can on the subject you're writing about.

Find a point during the day when you can comfortably jot down ideas, and immerse yourself in this information.

The creative process won't begin until you're eating, drinking and sleeping this research.

You can never know too much of one thing, and this may prove valuable information when you're trying to connect the dots.

5. Keep Your Inspiration Fires Burning

Make it a regular part of your writing work life to ensure your creative fires are burning. Create a notebook, make a file on your computer, or create a file full of marketing material to keep those creative juices going.

6. Big Things Have Small Beginnings

Where does a good idea come from? What does it look like?

It's very easy as a copywriter to bypass the small stuff and only look at bigger things. When in reality it's the small beginnings of an idea that are usually the best.

A simple tip to remember: learn to embrace all ideas, good, bad, small and even incredible. Even the most stupid idea that comes into your mind, write it all down.

Always sleep on it, and see what it looks like the next day.

Somewhere in that stack of ideas will be a really good one.

A copywriter's biggest problem is coming up with a masterpiece every time.

Creativity involves breaking out of expected patterns in order to look at things in a different way.

Edward de Bono.

7. Be Unconventional

Are you making the most of your weird ideas?

Unconventionality works together with creativity, seeing the world in a new light brings new creativity.

As children we're taught to conform and adapt, but not to be individuals. Thinking out of the box isn't something that you learn at school, that's why you need to tap into your creative side and bring it out.

There's no time like the present to embrace the weird and wonderful side of your creativity.

8. Throw Logic Out the Window

The copywriting arena requires writers to produce great

campaigns on tap. The best way to do this is to change your point of view, and play around with what you have.

You never know what you might come up with.

9. Go Outside

A blank computer screen will kill any creativity you might have. Routines are great, but there's nothing like taking a walk to blow the cobwebs away, and to get your creative inspiration going again.

The world can look completely different once you start discovering parts of your neighbourhood you've never visited before.

Any person in an industry that runs on creativity will tell you their best ideas came when they were experiencing life outside of the office, not when they were stuck at a desk.

10. You Don't Need to Start at the Beginning

As crazy as that sounds, you can start in the middle. You can write in the middle, even if it feels a bit strange, but you can always go back to the beginning and tie everything up properly.

11. Do Some Freewriting

Use freewriting and have a brainstorming session, all you have to do is write continuously. This can be about the product, or experience of trying to write about it. Or maybe you just want to get your thoughts of that moment on paper. The only thing that matters is that you put all of these thoughts and ideas out in the open on paper or on your computer.

Freewriting will literally free any thoughts locked away in your unconscious mind, some writers use this technique before they start their own writing session.

12. Sleep On It

Tapping into your unconscious mind can be a great help when you need to start your creative process. The easiest way to do this is to sleep on it.

Leave your thoughts and ideas to digest overnight and see what you come up with the next day. There's no harm in keeping a pen and paper by your bed, in case anything comes into your head while you're sleeping.

HOW TO CAPTIVATE YOUR READER

◆ ◆ ◆

Engage your reader by writing about everyday life using ordinary words, or illuminating them with a story.

What is engaging copy?

Being able to hold a conversation with your reader is what engaging copy is all about. You talk to readers one-on-one about things they might like, using their language, without talking down to them. Appreciating they're probably really busy, bored or tired. It's all about treating your reader the way you would like to be treated.

Communicate with your reader

Your copy will be read by thousands of people and is known in marketing as 'one to many' (a single source providing information to multiple people). Always remember to talk to your reader as an individual, instead of a group of people, the best copy works as a conversation between writer and reader. It can also work the opposite way, not unlike an uninterrupted correspondence, like an email from a manager to their workforce.

The way you address your reader can make or break your copy. You need to pull your reader into your copy by involving them in the conversation, just like you would talking to someone you know.

Always address your audience as individuals, instead of a collective, because most people are likely to be reading your text alone.

Write for the reader not the client

When you're working for a company it's only natural you're going to want to please the company, so you'll automatically start writing for the client because you want your copy to succeed. It's only normal to think about what they might want from you as a copywriter, and plus you hope for more projects from them in the future. What your client might have in mind may be completely wrong for the project.

Your reader should always be your primary focus on every project you deal with. So stop trying to impress your client with the copy, instead grab their attention with the thinking behind it.

Using copy that talks back

If you have an idea how your reader might respond, try talking back to them. In the summer of 2016 this technique was used to capitalise on the unfamiliarity of the product:

Kopparberg fruit lager.

Yeah, lager.

Using this in longer copy helps you build up a conversation with your reader, helping you answer their objections and questions as they arise. Here are a few examples:

Copy

The QR 2000 is the slimmest laptop you can buy.

Reader's thoughts

So what?

Copy

Pop into PC Planet any time to see it.

Reader's thoughts

I might just do that....

As you can see by the above examples this technique will give your copy both structure and flow. All you need to do is to decide where your reader is now and where you want them to finish, and use their expected responses to write the steps in between.

Why you should use 'we' or 'I' when you're writing copy

The best way to talk to the customer when writing for a company or brand, is to use 'we'. After all, you wouldn't talk about yourself in the third person would you? Things can start sounding really strange when that starts happening, so companies shouldn't do it either.

Write the way you speak

If copywriting is all about sounding like a conversation shouldn't it be written that way? Often this gets missed because some people think they should be writing in a certain way to get their message across. It's easy to hear what you want to say in your head, but when it comes to putting it down on paper it can sound too writerly, or finicky. The problem can be further worsened when the copywriter is asking the reader to do something, this is often taken the wrong way as authority instead of a simple formality.

Anyhow if you think you're beginning to sound too writerly, give your copy a more conversational rewrite, as novelist Elmore Leonard said, "If it sounds like writing, I rewrite it."

Shorter simpler sentences are used when you start writing like you talk, this should allow your copy to flow naturally and not sound clunky to the reader.

Would I say this out loud to someone?

Renowned adman Fairfax Cone used to ask copywriters, "Would you say that to someone you know?".

Some simple questions to ask yourself:

Would I say this out loud?

What would you think if someone said this to you?

How would you feel?

Another handy technique is to write for a friend or family member who might be using the product already.

Match the reader's language

The reader will gain a greater understanding of what you're trying to sell to them if you use the same language they use. This also demonstrates that you understand them, respect them, and like them. And also that reveals that you care about the conversation, and how much you really want it to work.

This can backfire if you start using jargon or language they don't understand. Giving the appearance of not caring anything about what the reader thinks.

Using big words can often put people off, when all they want is a product to a particular job. Use simple words, or better still Google it! Look on search engines and see what people are looking for.

Sometimes simplicity is all you need.

Take the reader's point of view

A great way to take the reader's point of view is to include some of the benefits of the product to their situation. Don't make your language abstract, keep it simple so they can get a clear picture of what it is they need to do.

Simple language is an uncomplicated way to connect with your audience who may have English as their first language, broadening your audience numbers.

Why you need to use verbs and not nouns in your copy

When you're using verbs in your copy you're using 'doing' words, making it easier for you to paint a picture in the reader's mind.

Noun phrases are often used and sound like a defence mechanism, putting people on a negative footing the moment they start reading your copy.

Your copywriting should always relate to your reader's concerns and not your own.

Bring it to life

Your job as a copywriter is to bring a product to life and make the reader want to buy it. You can do this by using sensory language: describing the sights, tastes, sounds, smells, and textures of using a product.

These sensory experiences go into our memories, and can often trigger strong emotions. Evoking the feeling of using a product, as well as physically experiencing it.

This kind of language can be used to show what the product may be like to use, with the help of a step-by-step guide.

Become a master of storytelling

A powerful tool in the copywriters arsenal is storytelling. Used by most copywriters for decades, stories are a way to make sense of the world. They can tap into the deepest memories, and emotions. Stories like those used in fairy tales prepare us for the life that lies ahead, and things we've yet to experience. Our memories, problems and emotions are spoken through stories. Our relationship with each other is also used in the same way, because stories are about life.

Some stories can be fantastical and take us to other places that are completely removed from our own experiences. When you start reading a story you're locked in and have to go with the story's flow. If we want to know the end of the story we have stuck through it the whole way.

Stories are more than just a technique of writing, they're something we all experience, and are different from digesting information about some product benefits, stories are one of a kind.

Storytelling is a good way to pass on information you want people to remember. They focus on real people, events, and emotions from real life which adds pathos to a message that might be a little dull. We learn from a very early age to listen to stories, which makes it an inherent part of us, making storytelling a very persuasive tool.

HOW TO POLISH YOUR COPY

◆ ◆ ◆

Polish your copy to make it shine.

The Importance of a Rewrite

Ernest Hemingway said, "All writing is rewriting", he knew exactly how hard it was to master the craft of writing, and how important the rewriting stage was.

Let's take a look as some important points that will be covered in this post:

Description - Are you serving a purpose with your descriptions? Is everything explained plainly in your copy?

Individual Words - Have you chosen the right words in your descriptions? Are your words easy to understand, or could you have used other words?

Phrases - Could you have used single words instead of a whole phrase? Is your wording obscure?

Sentences - Have you structured your sentences in a simple way? Are you using the passive voice?

Paragraphs - Do you use a new paragraph for a new idea? Are your paragraph breaks at a clear point in your copy?

Pace - Is your copy pace consistent throughout the text? If your pace changes is there a good reason for this?

Order - Is the order of your copy organised? Are you covering the main points of the product first, and the sub points later on?

Duplication - Is each part of your copy adding something unique in terms of advantages? Have you repeated the same point more than once in your copy?

Focus - Is your theme clear throughout your copy? Does your headline feature throughout your copy?

Length - Have you stuck to your points succinctly? Have you given your readers information to get them to where you want them to be?

Make it Plain - Keep your language clear and plain.

Let's get started.

Simple is Always Better

1. Uncomplicated words are fundamental

When we start learning to read and write we always start with the easy words, and these words stay with us throughout our lives.

2. Clear words are dependable

You can depend on clear straightforward language that is fuss-free.

3. Easy words are truthful

Trust is built through persuasion, which is why easy words come across as the most honest.

4. Straightforward language is the clearest

Research has shown that readers see writers who write simply as more intelligent and not less. By writing in clear language you help to solidify ideas into the minds of your readers.

5. Uncomplicated words are easier to understand

People grasp simpler language more quickly, showing the writer cares about the reader.

6. Easy words are universal

You reach a wider audience if you use simple language. Which means that a reader is more likely to take action, which is the endgame for all copywriters.

Your audience will never know how many rewrites have been done to produce an easy-to-read piece of copy.

You might be thinking that it's easy to write simple and clearly off the bat. Messy first drafts are the order of the day when it comes to copywriting. Words will start coming in no particular order and will sound really mixed. Every copy has the job of making the complicated look effortless.

You need a clear mind to write simply, and a deep understanding of your subject matter. That means you have to do thorough research on each product. Gathering enough knowledge to know what will benefit the reader. Being able to say enough to convince the reader to buy the product.

With each key headline introduce an essential element about the product. Developing the idea through each paragraph. You only need to express things once. Making every word count, and not overdoing it by using too many sentences.

When you edit your copy look at it the same as you would if you were pruning a rose bush. Only leave in the valuable stuff.

Writing short and pithy sentences are even more valuable for copy online. Because of the limited amount of space you may have to get your message across.

A good guide to go by is using too much punctuation in a sentence, even once punctuation is excessive.

Choose words that are familiar, and not ambiguous, this is particularly useful to people who use English as their second or third language.

Variety is the name of the game, which means good copy should contain a variety of words, and sentences, otherwise it'll come across quite dull to the audience.

Kill Your Darlings (Get Rid of the Things You Love the Most)

Simply put this means that you shouldn't fall in love with your ideas. This rings true more than ever in the copywriting process. When you come up with ideas you just have to include them in your text. As time rolls on you're convincing yourself it has to stay, even though it's not in the brief. Which is why you need to "Kill your darlings."

The endgame is to please the client, not yourself. If your copy isn't doing the job of persuading the reader it's got to go.

Your perspective starts to dim the longer you work on a project. That's why sometimes it's a good idea to show your copy to someone trustworthy you know and ask them to show your "darlings".

If you feel like your copy has ticked all the boxes of the brief, then chances are they have.

If your creativity kicks in and you feel you have an idea that meets the pitch perfectly, then you need to fight for it.

Stay Tangible

When you're writing copy it's easy to start at ground level writing all of the real advantages a product has. But if you're working on the project for too long you start adding things that have no tangible benefits at all, and you start writing things just to make the audience feel good.

All products benefit people in one way or another. Your problem is, are you writing something worthwhile for the reader?

Easy on the Verbs

Description is a good thing in copywriting, the only problem is the way you use it. You need to be more selective when it comes to choosing your adjectives and adverbs. The most commonly used adjectives such as 'simple', 'new' and 'unique' hold the most value when it comes to articulating the important benefits of a product. Throwing in a little sensory detail doesn't do any harm either, like 'tender steak' instead of just 'steak'.

If you're struggling to find the right words use a thesaurus. Sometimes we forget how many words there are to choose from that will help to describe what we want to say.

Top copywriter Tony Brignull says "Treat adjectives and adverbs as if they cost £500 each". To use this measure ask yourself if you would pay to leave in each adverb and adjective used in your copy. If you would, that's great, but if not, turn them into verbs.

The Debate Over Long and Short Copy

Long-copy followers would tell you that longer is best. On the other side of the fence are the microcopy producers, or short copy disciples who create content for social media platforms who are avid users of short copy because it's more in tune and akin to current times.

You could argue it's more about making progress and moving with the times. That long copy is old hat, and short copy is in. Some would even argue the attention span of people has reduced significantly and that's why short copy is the best.

These days both are going strong, and for the most part people like to read what interests them the most. Your audience's attention span is valuable and should therefore never be wasted. These days people don't spend their time telling advertising companies that their adverts are too long. Writing long copy can be useful especially when it's something interesting or worth reading. There's no such thing as long copy if it keeps your reader absorbed from the get go.

All you need to know is that your copy needs to be long enough to get your readers to where you want them to be, which is buying the product.

Pacing Your Copy

Fiction writing is a good example of how pacing is used in writing, using a faster pace for thrillers, and a slow lingering one for a romantic novel.

The pace you choose all depends on what you want to achieve, and the experience you want to generate. If you're writing about a fast food chain you want something snappy and straight to the point. But with a high end restaurant you might want to say something at a more measured speed deliberating over the more relaxed experience.

Using that opportunity to create a particular kind of mood or ambience. This kind of copy is used in charity advertising where a particular circumstance is used to ask the audience for help. If you can keep the reader's curiosity, their empathy will start to deepen and your call to action will become more powerful.

Find Your Rhythm

Most people don't speak in a monotone drone, they'll use certain syllables, or place more emphasis on certain words. If you listen closely you can hear how their voices change for loudness and the use of longer vowels. They'll also pause between certain, which is where punctuation is used in writing.

When you read something, you're listening to the words in your head as if they're being spoken to you. If you want to sound more persuasive to your reader you need your words and sentences to sound right. When you're writing in conversational style it needs to sound the same as everyday speak. To the reader your copy should have a pleasant pattern of stressed and unstressed syllables. Giving your reader a nice mix of long and short words, just enough to let them draw breath as they read your copy.

Make Your Words Rhyme

Psychologists have found that people see rhyming statements as 22% more accurate than non-rhyming ones. Which is why you often see it in advertising slogans.

Once you pop you can't stop.

A memorable rhyme from Pringles perfectly describes a common belief of what might emerge when you eat something good.

Use Alliteration in Your Sentences and Copy

Most major brands have used alliteration in their copy at one point or another over the years.

Here are a few examples of brand names, sports teams, and characters that all use alliteration:

PayPal

Range Rover

Circuit City

LA Lakers

KKR

Pittsburgh Pirates

Tic-tac

King Kong

Peter Parker

Bruce Banner

Alliterations aren't essential to your brand, but they will help carry your message further if you can include them in your copy.

The reasoning behind this is to do with the use of repetition. Repeated and regular linguistic cues are one of the best ways to create big, predictable results.

Use a Fresh Set of Eyes to Check Your Copy Over

Mistakes become harder to see the longer you work on a piece of copy. It's not the job of the client to pick up on things you might have missed. This is why you have to check your work meticulously to make sure you haven't missed anything or left anything out.

Often it's best to have a hard copy print out to check for any mistakes you might have missed. It also helps to leave a little time in between writing your copy to check it over.

If you can't get someone you know to have a look through it for you, hire a professional proofreader to do the work for you.

MASTERING THE ART OF PERSUASION

❖ ❖ ❖

Strategies to persuade your readers.

You don't need to be the world's greatest grammarian to write copy that sells, in this chapter we're going to look at strategies that will persuade your reader, while improving your writing. Empowering you to write copy that captivates your reader to take action and buy what you're selling.

Writing great copy is the ability to write really well, and being able to connect with your audience clearly communicating your message.

Here is a list of copywriting strategies to take your writing from good to great, and help you close more sales:

Highlight Advantages Over Features

For no apparent reason most copywriters tend to write about the features of a product instead of the real benefits the product can give. The problem with this is it holds no real appeal with customers. Features are required at the correct time to show readers what's included in the product, but they don't persuade the customer to buy what you're selling. The benefits of a product are much more credible at convincing customers to buy the product.

More commonly than not the features or technical aspects of a product end up confusing the reader, and only appeal to a select, hardcore group of consumers.

As far as copywriting goes, you need to highlight the benefits first, your goal being to steer your copy with benefits at the beginning of your copy, then go on to list the features.

Be as Accurate as Possible

Making general claims about a product is easy to do, but bringing in solid proof is much more effective.

Throwing in general numbers and claims are too good to be true and can seem unbelievable to customers. Ask yourself if you would believe the claims you're making.

What should you do instead?

This is why you should be as accurate about your claims as possible. Use real information and numbers about the product you're selling. Those numbers are more credible and look less likely like they've been made up.

Putting in that extra work and research about the products sold will make your copy more effective. Think about anything else that will help you to sell to customers. Can you include case studies where consumers have saved $X of dollars or grew their business by X%? If that is the case be sure to feature these benefits in your copy.

Use Emotion in Your Copy

Most people are heavily persuaded by their emotions. Most people think they buy something because it's a logical purchase, but the reality is your emotions are stronger than you think, and that is why your emotions guide you to your purchase.

When it comes to decision making, your emotions are never far behind. Your arguments for purchasing something can seem rational, but you miss out the most important part of the brain you need to target.

Creating copy is about tapping into the customer's emotions, and making them understand that the purchase will improve a part of their life and solve a problem.

By increasing the emotional appeal you create a desire in your reader for what you're selling.

Learn How to Use Real Testimonials to Your Benefit

The credibility a testimonial can give to a product is like finding gold at the end of a rainbow. Because testimonials are so important in selling a product, they bring the company untold authenticity. Anything you say to a reader can be taken with a grain of salt, but add a testimonial and it solidifies something that it is true.

Sharing testimonials from real customers puts your company's credibility up by 100% with the customer, because this shows how trustworthy your product is.

Testimonials are a useful tool for increasing believability, and being able to express something you wouldn't ordinarily be able to say. That is why so many websites and companies use testimonials on their websites to sell their products.

Here are some quick examples of when you can use testimonials in your copy:

1. Enable you to say things you can't say

2. Reinforcing key aspects of your copy

3. Feature important clients

4. Used to create headlines

Don't Make Your Copy All About You

This goes without saying if you're working for any client, but is just as important if you're creating copy for your own blog or website.

A lot of businesses use business-centric copy instead of customer-centric. Writing about how wonderful their product is but forgetting the customer, and what their needs are.

Customers only care about what you can do for them, they look for things that fit the problem they have, or something to help them accomplish their goals.

That's why all of your copy should be customer-centric.

Use a Conversational Tone in Your Copy

The conversational tone of writing is more personable, and is an easier way of getting your message across to your audience.

You should never sound like you're more important than your audience, this will put your readers off straight away. Your copy should always feel like they're talking to a person. So make your copy concise, to the point, and get your message across in as few words as possible.

Create Copy that Compels the Reader to Want More

Each sentence you write should wet your reader's appetite.

Readers should be left wanting to know more about the product, and how it can benefit them in their lives.

This starts with the headline, a headline should prompt your audience enough to read the next sentence, and so on.

All of your sentences and paragraphs should be cleverly orchestrated and flow as you read them. All of your words should be necessary, and every sentence should operate in propelling the reader forward.

How do you write copy that compels the audience?

Your reader should be your priority at all times. Ask yourself if at any point the reader would be bored by what they're reading? Are they interested in what I have to say?

Your main focus should be on the reader's needs, desires and interests.

Always remember to write as much as you need to, and no more. Do you think your points strengthen your copy, or bring your audience any closer to purchasing the product?

Write Faster

Writing faster may seem totally illogical, but it will help you to write more effective copy.

How will this make my copy more effective?

1. Writing quickly utilises the emotional side of your brain. Rather than rewriting on the spot your copy is flowing from the way you feel about the subject matter. Which is good for writing persuasive copy, because it will help you to appeal to your readers' emotions.

2. It's easier to improve what's already there than to write a perfect first draft. Editing and rewriting improves the way your copy feels, instead of spending endless hours trying to write a perfect first draft.

The main thing to remember is to get your ideas down on paper. After you've written it out you can edit it to your heart's content. The finished article will be a well-polished piece of copy.

Don't Use Overly Complicated Language in Your Copy

Simple is best.

This comes from the belief that the average reading level is between the 7th and 8th grade. It's probable that most of your audience will read at this level.

If you make things too complicated you'll quickly start to lose your reader. This could be because of complex sentence structure or using complex vocabulary.

You never want to alienate your readers, instead you should be choosing words that most people will know and understand.

Keep Your Paragraphs Short

This applies more than ever to online copy, because shorter paragraphs are easier to digest and read online.

A study conducted in 2004 (the Eyetrack III Study) conducted by the Poynter Institute stated that shorter paragraphs received twice as many fixations as long ones. Meaning, that people prefer shorter paragraphs than longer ones.

If you're writing copy for traditional sales print, this doesn't matter so much. Online is a different story, they help to break up text and make your copy less daunting.

Hire a Professional Editor

As a writer you've probably realised by now that you can't pick up every mistake you make. A lot of this is to do with the fact that you're too close to your work, and will be more subjective because it's your own work.

The biggest problem with typos is they slowly erode your credibility. Too many errors in your work can result in your readers not taking you seriously, or worse still you could end up losing clients.

An experienced editor who deals with copywriters all of the time will know the kind of mistakes to look out for. Things you would miss a lot of the time.

If you can't afford a professional editor or proofreader, let one of your close friends or family look over your work for you. There's nothing wrong with a fresh set of eyes, and plus it won't undermine your credibility.

Show the Value of Your Product

Customers looking for a good deal always want to know that their money is being spent wisely.

Your main aim is to show the value of your product, you do this by demonstrating why they'll be getting a good deal when they purchase what you're selling.

By following these points you'll become better prepared to write copy that persuades your audience and compels your customers to take decisive action.

HOW TO USE PSYCHOLOGY TO ENGAGE, INFLUENCE AND SELL

◆ ◆ ◆

Make use of your audience's selective perception and biases to alter their perspective.

Persuasion or Manipulation?

Getting to the truth can be a huge hurdle for most humans, at the best of times. Causing our brains to suffer from severe mental perception, biases, distortions and omissions that can clash with our reality. This becomes even worse when we start trying to compare things such as cost, size or probability of a product. However, for a copywriter these shortcomings can be used in ways to give your copy some extra elevation.

The following points could be seen as a fine line between manipulation or persuasion, and it's up to you whether you feel they should be used in your copy.

Ten Extremely Persuasive Copywriting Techniques

1. Distinction Bias

Distinction bias is viewing two as more distinctive when evaluating them simultaneously than when evaluating them separately (Wikipedia).

The alternate product offered doesn't need to exist in the real world, all it has to do is be of less value than whatever you're selling at the time. By choosing the grounds of comparison to suit your plan.

For example:

Thriftyheat provides four different ways to programme your heating - most controllers have just three.

Ideally customers should be querying how many heating programming methods are adequate, and if the number is relevant at all. However, if you give them two options, one of which is inferior to yours, they'll go for the best offer every time.

2. The Double Bind

The reality of a double bind is that both alternatives lead to the same place. For example:

Order online, or call by our store to browse and buy a selection of our sofas.

The reader is presented with two choices, but each ultimately ends in a purchase. The objective is to offer the customer options that are two levels of behaviour. How to purchase, and make a purchase, both representing the same thing. Not buying the product is not included by suggestion.

3. The Forer Effect

Bertram Forer, a psychologist, gave a group of students what they thought was a personal profile, but was actually a list of 13 statements that were identical for all of them. But the students still marked the personal profile 4.26 out of 5 for accuracy, for the most part.

Because the statements were so vague, it was clear that just about anyone could identify with them.

For example:

You have an intense desire to get people to accept and like you.

Sometimes you give too much effort on projects that don't work out.

You can be overly harsh on yourself and very critical.

Some of Forer's most common statements began with 'At times...' Because people don't have personality types, but rather personality states.

Therefore if you're trying to build empathy with your audience, it's much more effective to tap into something they've probably thought or felt at some point in time, instead of trying to squeeze them into a persona.

4. The Endowment Effect

The endowment effect is the tendency to overvalue what they own. This means people would prefer to pay extra for something they already own, than get the same article from someone else. This is because people feel loss when they give up something they already have, and people don't like losing their own stuff. And they dislike rational thinking even more.

The endowment effect is used regularly in time-limited trials, test drives, free-to-play video games etc. It makes sense when you think about it, all of the aforementioned things are to hook the audience, and make the product feel like it's already theirs. Even if money hasn't exchanged hands.

5. Authority

Getting people to buy something can seem like an uphill struggle at the best of times. When you bring authority into the equation it changes everything.

Most people will already be familiar with the authority you cite, but regardless, all you need to give them is an official-sounding title or qualification.

For example:

Top dentists recommend Regenerate toothpaste.

Most people won't bother to question the authority you're putting over to them. This trick has been used by countless copywriters throughout the decades.

6. Embedded Commands

An embedded command is a sentence within a sentence, taking the form of an imperative.

For example:

You can visit our store anytime between 10am and 6pm.

The sentence sounds more easy-going and relaxed, and less pushy to the audience.

7. Reactance

This is doing the opposite of what we're told, even when it may be beneficial to us.

For example:

You probably won't believe this, but Energylight broadband could be ten times faster than your current broadband user.

Using reactance, the reader is goaded into 'proving you wrong', daring them to not believe, when they went ahead and believed it anyway.

8. Using Partial Claims

Trying to make a product sound credible with a claim can be really difficult, especially if the product isn't that great. However, there is a way to get around this by using a partial claim.

For example:

Hair Renew decreases hair loss

and

Hair Renew helps to minimise hair loss

You would think they sound the same, but if you look closer Hair Renew takes all the credit, but you could liken the second sentence to a toddler doing the washing up.

9. Vague Numbers Equal Zero Promises

Cold hard data can give your copy a much needed boost, but this only works if the data makes sense.

This is where you can use 'up to', helping you to create a big-sounding claim without saying anything at all.

Root Base reduces persistent weeds by up to 75%

When you use 'up to 75%' it simply means that Root Base weedkiller will only get rid of between 0% and 75%, which isn't really a promise. But what it is doing is giving a vague indication of an undefined benefit that sounds really good.

When you tell people their results will be somewhere within a percentage range they'll always assume their results will be near the top.

10. Anchoring

You might be writing copy for a product that doesn't sound too bad, but the price is dubious.

If you can bring a big number into your copy, every other number offered to your audience will sound small in comparison.

For instance, if you're selling mattresses, you talk about the premier model mattress which costs upwards of $800. But when you reveal your low price mattress from Dormant at 'just' $400, your product starts to sound acceptable.

For all your audience knows, your number could have been pulled out of a hat.

Even when a premium mattress can cost upwards of $800, the Dormant mattress comes in at a moderate $400.

HOW TO HIT THE RIGHT TONE

♦ ♦ ♦

Craft the right tone across all of your copy.

Personality of a Brand, or Tone of Voice

The way we talk reflects our personality, the same applies to a product brand.

Brands are no different, the words they use reflect the personality of a brand. The audience you're targeting will connect with the tone you choose, and this will help to convey the brand's consistency, character and value.

Let's dig a little deeper.

1. Consistency

In order to paint a clear picture for the reader there needs to be consistency all the way through the copy. If the tone changes frequently, people will quickly switch off, and start to forget it.

All marketing channels, products, ads, and campaigns must have the same consistent message and tone throughout. You can change marketing campaigns, but you can't change the brand's voice.

That's why all brands carry their visual identity with them, using consistent typography, symbols, colour and imagery through everything they produce.

The way the brand looks is just as important as it sounds to the consumer. Companies use their branding everywhere these days, from the stationery in an office, to the signs used in the staff car park. It shows the audience and staff that the company brand has one cohesive voice.

2. Character

If people don't remember a brand, it's usually because they don't like the way it sounds. But with a consistent tone of voice, you can start to express the brand's unique personality.

Effective copy will utilise creative ideas, and offer appealing writing to make a product stand out from the crowd more. With the right tone of voice the reader will be engaged because the brand is showing an interesting personality they can connect with. Which means they'll listen to it whenever they watch an ad campaign or read an ad in a newspaper.

People will go out of their way to listen to a brand's message. This couldn't be more clear than when a company, such as John Lewis, a well-known British brand, releases their Christmas ad campaign.

The brands we choose to buy from are the ones we are more likely to tune into, because we enjoy what the brand has to say.

This doesn't mean the brand will be popular with everyone, it just means we've identified the right audience.

3. Value

A brand that consistently conveys likability, will also communicate value. This means the reader trusts the voice they're listening to. This kind of brand offers its audience valuable products that are reliable and have long-lasting selling power.

A brand makes a promise to its consumers, the tone of voice

ensures that message gets across consistently irrespective of the situation, time or product.

A brand is more than a logo or slogan, it's how the audience perceives the brand that gives them their marketability.

A company needs everything to work together, in order to give its audience an experience they'll remember, and keep coming back for. Creating the right tone is still an important part of the branding process, because it will help bring in new customers, and keep the loyal ones happy too.

Investigating Brand Character

The things we say reflect our personality, and the same can be said of any brand. Which is why you need to set the right tone. To do this you need to look into the brand's personality and what it stands for.

Begin by looking at the brand as a person. And start asking questions like:

What kind of a personality do they have?

What are their values?

How do they run their business?

What are their friends like?

What kind of clothes do they like?

What does their house look like?

Do they have any hobbies or interests?

What's their favourite food?

All of these questions reveal a lot about someone's personality, and this is no different to a brand's personality. Use these questions to write your own character summary.

Use a Human Voice

If you want a brand to stand-out from the crowd it needs to have its own voice, and not sound like every other corporate entity out there. You can reach an audience much quicker if you don't like everyone else.

Start asking yourself questions like:

What is the brand passionate about?

What problems do they solve?

How can they help the consumer?

Get to know more about the founder of the company, start looking into the way the company is run, and how the offices are furnished. This will give you a real sense of what the company's personality is about.

Be Truthful

The tone you use needs to be a true reflection of what the reader will expect when they buy the product. Instead people will become less convinced of what the brand has to offer.

Brand Values

This is the core of what the brand stands for, and how it will help the customer. All of these characteristics should permeate throughout the brands ad campaigns and newsletters etc.

Not every brand has their values set in stone. Whatever the situation you need to know this before you can decide on the right tone.

You should be able to define a brand's values by about three to five different characteristics. If the brand you're writing for happens to have 'understated' or 'modest' as part of their values, they won't want those thrown around in public. Some values show through in what you don't say.

Creating the Right Tone of Voice

Now that you've sorted out the brand's values, you need to use them to set the foundation for the tone you'll be using.

Some Other Useful Tips on Finding the Right Tone

It's also useful to look at other human characteristics in order to help you describe the right tone.

For example:

How long has the brand been around?

Is the brand more suited to men or women, or is it universal?

Where does the brand come from? Does it have English as its first language?

Did the brand start in a particular time period?

Use a different culture or brands to describe your tone in broader terms.

Tone of Voice Rules

Some companies may have already chosen their tone of voice, and have it already recorded in a document for you to look through. These guidelines will help you to write consistently throughout any project you work on for that particular company.

If you've worked for the same company more than once, you've probably built up a tone of voice with that particular company, so you may not need to write down a set of values.

Or maybe you find that the more you write about a product the more the tone comes through.

HINTS AND TIPS FOR VARIOUS PROJECTS

◆ ◆ ◆

Copywriting tips for various projects.

We're going to look at four different project areas you're more likely to work on. Everything suggested below are just hints and tips to consider, while some maybe dos and don'ts.

Blogs and Websites

Give each page a clear theme and purpose. For pages that are too busy, split them up, and combine pages that look like they're duplicate. And delete pages with no real purpose.

For each page write an informative headline that explains the purpose of the page for the benefit of search engines and the audience.

Make your message clear when you're writing for business websites, while taking into consideration that any page may be a landing page when visitors stumble across the site.

It's not very likely that people will read every page of the website, but each page should be able to work on its own.

Break up the copy with subheadings, because most people will skim, or scroll around the page. Subheadings should be convincing as well as descriptive.

Making your page of text is interesting by breaking it up into columns, bullets, tables and subheadings.

Use a structure like a family tree so people that skim through the page will get the most important information first.

Keep your sentences short and snappy because people read information from the phones and tablets.

Write pages that include all of the necessary information for the reader. For instance, home pages are there to guide the audience, product pages tell the reader what they need to know about the product.

Products and services should be written from the reader's point of view, evoking the experience of using the product.

Emails

Write copy that target's your audience, if you're using an email list. Tell your audience what they want to know, and what they should do next.

Treat your subject line like a headline.

Create intrigue with 'How', 'How to', 'Why' or 'What'. Giving your readers something valuable like a human-interest story related to the product.

Make the email personal with the person's name in the salutation.

Use everyday words to connect with the reader, just like you would if you were talking to a friend.

Short copy will work better in an email, so you need to get to the point as soon as the email is opened.

Make your call-to-action clear, and logical, using a problem, solution, benefits or proof using phrases to connect the reader from sentence to the next, keeping them engaged.

Sales Letters

All of the points mentioned below can be applied to longer copy or freestanding copy that is designed to take readers from their initial curiosity to purchase.

Throughout the letter refer to the user as 'you', and yourself as 'I' or 'we'. to demonstrate the communication is personal. Start the salutation with the reader's first name 'Dear John'.

Make the time to get your headline right, because if it doesn't sound right, everything that follows will seem immaterial.

Write a headline that's aimed at the reader, introduce a problem or solution, then offer the main benefit of the product.

Create an opening that's as detailed and appealing, showing the audience you understand their feelings and current situation. Relate the problem, explaining why it's a huge challenge to the customer.

Tell the reader what will happen if they don't act now, and continue down the same path.

Present the problem as the solution to their dilemma, and how it will tackle all parts of the problem mentioned beforehand. Use social proof and real testimonials to bring other voices to strengthen your case.

Concentrate on the reader's anxiety about buying, responding or donating, and use it to make their desire stronger than their objection.

Use a call-to-action to ask for a sale, with clear instructions of what they need to do. Tell them it's easy to process, and may include a free trial or money-back offer.

Social Media Posts

These tips are suited to content published on social media platforms such as Facebook and Twitter.

Always take into consideration the reader's situation, they didn't ask for your message, and they may not even engage with everything posted.

Your headline on Twitter should have a theme, offer a benefit, sound intriguing, ask a question or give the reader some news.

Commands can be used as powerful calls-to-action.

Be careful who you link to, and make sure you deliver the audience the promise you gave them in the post you've written.

Keep your posts short and simple, to help cut through all of the noise.

Offer your readers value with your posts, give them something that will be of great benefit to them.

Make it visual, and relatable, with a good representation of what you're saying.

Talk in a positive, active and concrete voice using words they would use.

Your social media posts should sound the same as any other copy you do for that particular brand.

TOOLS

TOOLS AND RESOURCES TO MAKE YOUR LIFE SIMPLER

◆ ◆ ◆

All writers and copywriters alike have their own particular box of tricks to pull from.

I've gathered together a list that covers every aspect of copywriting, from language and grammar, research, to copywriting tone of voice.

Legal Stuff

Useful legal materials for copywriters. The legal know-how that lets you know what's involved in the legal process of copywriting.

GDPR FAQs for sending cold emails

Everything you need to know about GDPR compliance.

ASA rulings

Learn how the CAP Code works by reading the ASA rulings. A new batch is published every Wednesday, and straight to your inbox if you want it. Your eyes will be opened when you see how many brands break the rules.

The CAP Code

You need to know your boundaries off by heart when you start claiming what a product can do. The CAP Code will fill you in.

Images and Photos

Believe it or not copywriters working online need to brighten up their posts with images.

Images for social media

An up-to-date guide on social media image sizes from *Sprout Social*.

33 brilliant sources for free images

Thoughtfully has done the groundwork for you already, discover what the websites have to offer in the way of royalty-free images.

Special Typography (Diacritics and special characters)

Typography is a key element of copywriting and getting it right is half the battle.

Cut-and-paste diacritics

Typeit is an easy-to-use platform for choosing your language or characters, and pasting them straight into your word processor.

Tables of character codes

Discover a comprehensive list of characters, listed alphabetically which includes codes for PCs, Macs, and HTML.

Scroll-through list of letters and diacritics

Toptal gives you a list of HTML Letter Symbols, Letter Entities and ASCII Letter Character Code Reference.

Scroll-through maths and science symbols and codes

A further list from Toptal in an easy-to-read format.

List of logic symbols

A well organised list from Wikipedia.

Currency symbols and codes

If you're not sure about what currency symbol to use for the Aruba Gilder or Brazil Real XE gives you the symbols, codes and simple alternative three-letter code.

Three-letter currency codes

IBAN gives you the full list of three letter currency codes which you won't find in the about XE list.

Text wizard's special characters guide

This resource covers the entire topic, and more. Including a list of definitions, instructions for tapping alt-codes, and Unicode straight into Word.

Bypassing Spam Filters

See whether your email copy will get through spam filters with some help from these links.

Huge list of filter-spooking words

Discover which words and phrases could cause you problems with Automantional's 475-wordlist.

The ultimate list of filter-spooking words

Find out which words will get you into trouble with Karen Rubin's Hubspot list.

Inspiration Generators

Looking for inspiration? Often all it takes is a bump in the right direction.

Title generator

If you're really desperate for a clickbait headline look no further.

Headline generator

Does the same job as the one above, with the added advantage of being able to tailor your custom-fit your selection depending on the type of content you're writing.

Refine your headline

Sign up and drop your headline into the CoSchedule analyser for an instant evaluation.

Polish your email subject line

Get openability subject lines from CoSchedule with no nonsense text that scores brilliantly.

Reverse-engineered marketing and copywriting inspiration

Delve into a huge resource of ads that have worked for other copywriters at one time or another. There may be a nugget waiting to be dug out for your next copywriting project.

Find a quote about a topic

Search by topic with Quoteland.

Search for listings on anything

From entertainment, music, nerdy stuff, sports, living, history, culture, the skies the limit on Ranker for lists on anything.

Grammar and Language

There's no need for any self-assured writer or copywriter to be paying for a premium grammar service checker online.

But if you're looking for a safeguard against anyone who thinks your writing isn't following the grammar rule book, here are some helpful pages for you to look at.

Grammar checker number 1

Grammarly, a heavily promoted grammar checker and resource. The free version isn't up to much, and the premium begs the question as to whether you really need to use it all.

Grammar checker number 2

Scribens is about the best online grammar checker on the list. It has the added advantage of accepting more text than most of the others.

Online Oxford Dictionary

Even really great writers need to check their spelling every now and again.

The Urban Dictionary

Urban dictionary was started for everyone to share their language. Originally intended to subvert the authority of the traditional dictionary. Created to document our messy, weird, and unpredictable language as it evolves.

"Yes, you can start a sentence with and"

A website killing the myth that you can't start a sentence with the word "and".

The Oxford Comma: Use it or Ditch it?

The pros and cons of using the Oxford Comma from proofreadnow.

Wordhippo

A favourite word tool of mine.

Timesavers - Text to Speech - Speech to Text

A time-saving tool with the ability to turn speech into text, and text into speech. The first lowers time transcribing, and the latter helps to clear out awkward phrases. Good for any kind of writing - particularly video scripts and speeches.

Microsoft text to speech

Word can be set up to read your text back to you. It will only read what's on the page. You can get a free Chrome extension if you use Google Docs.

Convert spoken word into text

Otter is a handy tool to record interviews or record case studies and automatically turn them into text. Sign up for free and get 600 minutes a month.

Improve documentation productivity and get more done

A life-saver for any writer that doesn't want to type. This handy piece of kit allows you to control your entire desktop with your voice.

Get Up to Speed With these Copywriting Glossaries

Learn the jargon of marketing and copywriting with these glossaries.

The A-Z of typographic terms

With simple explanations Fontsmith is a joy to read and discover.

Technology terms

This comprehensive list comes courtesy of WhatIs.

Marketing terms and definitions

TheBalance explains each term with a mini essay, not like many dictionaries that seem to be more of a patchwork affair.

Plagiarism

It's good to know if you're reading someone else's copy that they haven't taken the easy route (cheating) to create the perfect copy.

Plagiarism checker

Small SEO Tools provides you with a percentage value for plagiarism and originality.

Readability

Make life easier for your readers.

Readability measures

Discover the many scales of calculating readability.

Check your content for readability

Another useful tool from Readable, simply copy and paste your text and get a speedy result.

Test the readability of your webpages

An easy way to make sure another copywriter's work is fit for purpose.

The Hemingway App

The best free readability checker around.

Research

All copywriters should know their facts.

Academic papers

Google Scholar provides an almost limitless amount of research.

Statistics

Get stats about just about everything from Pew Research Centre.

Multiple searches

Get all of your online search options on one page with refdesk.

Internet archive on the Wayback Machine

The Wayback machine will bring up information from websites that have been saved over time.

Editing and proofreading

Some useful shortcuts and techniques to help you along.

Converting text from PDFs

Ever wondered how to extract text from a PDF to edit or read it? Lorraine Williams discovered a way to export PDF text in its entirety straight to Google Docs or Word.

Airtight proofreading

Textwizard's foolproof proofreading steps to clean your copy.

Formulas

The sequence of copywriting elements that leads a customer to the sale, is probably most well-known with the AIDA formula.

The Ultimate Guide to No-Pain Copywriting

Copyhackers has put together probably one of the most comprehensive lists I've seen online.

Tone of voice

Most of the time the tone of voice is speculation or just a gut feeling.

HELEN BOLAM

Find your voice

Voicebox is a radically simple approach to defining a brand's tone of voice.

AFTERWORD

◆ ◆ ◆

Thank you for reading *The Indispensable Guide to Copywriting: How to Write Effective and Compelling Copy That Sells*. I hope you enjoyed this book. If you did...

1. Help other people find this by writing a review.
2. Visit my website **1976write.com**.
3. Sign up for my Substack at **1976write**.
4. Visit my social media:

Twitter: **@1976write**
LinkedIn: **Helen Bolam**
Tumblr: **1976write**
Pinterest: **1976write**

Or read more of my books on Amazon by searching for Helen Bolam.

And if you have a moment, please review *The Indispensable Guide to Copywriting: How to Write Effective and Compelling Copy That Sells*. online. Help other like-minded readers and tell them why you enjoyed reading.

Thank you very much!

www.ingramcontent.com/pod-product-compliance
Lightning Source LLC
Chambersburg PA
CBHW070657220526
45466CB00001B/477